WATCHMAKING MADE EASY

1

An Illustrative and Descriptive Guide with Amazing Pictures on How to Make Watches with Ease

Dave John

Table of Contents

CHAPTER ONE

INTRODUCTION

Everybody put on watches. Be that as it may, it is very uncommon to go over individuals who make proficient watches. This is ordinarily because of somewhat expanded mechanization in the business achieving less watchmakers approaching into the workforce. There is anyway still an energetic age that wants to see new watchmakers ascend with incredible potential. You become a watchmaker either through apprenticeship, or setting off to a watch making school.

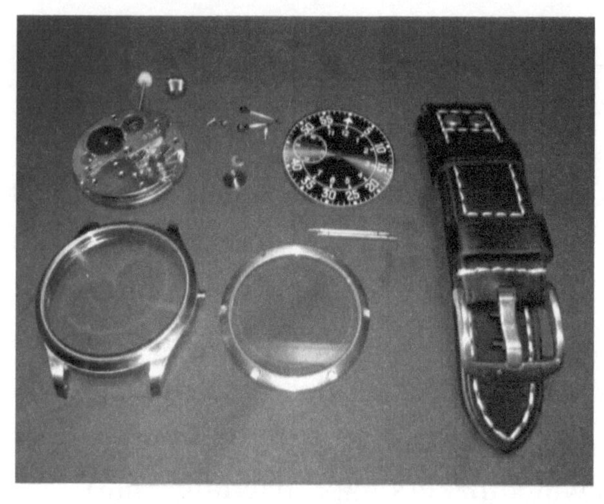

CHAPTER TWO

TIPS FOR LEARNING THE SKILLS OF WATCH MAKING

1. You can start by taking in the nuts and bolts from home. Prior to turning into an understudy, you can settle on developing your insight into watch making perfectly. Your expansive information on watchmaking will make you progressively employable. Take a stab at dismantling of a watch that you wouldn't fret in the event that it gets harm. At that point, take a stab at assembling it once more. This may assist you with understanding the life systems of a watch. Likewise take a stab at drawing charts and making takes note of that you can allude to even as you reassemble the watch.

2.	Try retaining various sorts of watch casing. A few watch faces are round fit as a fiddle. This shape is normally known as a watch packaging. Watch housings can anyway be delivered to take various shapes, for example, square shapes, circles, ovals, or squares. These shapes can be anything but difficult to learn, yet anyway you should have a broad information on other basic sorts of watch housings too.

CHAPTER THREE

KINDS/TYPES OF WATCH CASING

- Carriage watch casing: They resemble a circle that has been crunched deep down.

- Tonneau Watch Casings: They seem, by all accounts, to be bended by the sides yet anyway directly at top and the base.

- Carre Watch Casings: They have a bended top and base yet it is straight by the sides.

- Synthetic sapphire gem packaging

- Mineral gem packaging

- Acrylic gem.

3.   You ought to likewise have the option to recognize the precious stone covering on the essence of the watch. All watches are comprised of a slender precious stone layer covering the outside of the watch. The most generally utilized watch packaging types are the manufactured sapphire precious stone, mineral gem, and acrylic gem.

Sapphire is an extremely hard and solid material, bested uniquely by the precious stone. Watchmakers generally utilize lab to integrate sapphire to use its regular hardness. This gem could be over the top expensive, however extreme.

Mineral precious stone anyway is a type of glass. It is generally economical. Be that as it may, the material effectively gets scratches, and it can't be polished out. Mineral precious stone must be supplanted so as to show up new once more.

Acrylic precious stone is anyway the least expensive type of gem covering. It is produced using plastic and can scratch without any problem. A portion of the acrylic gem scratches can without much of a stretch be polished out. It is really the most vulnerable gem ever.

4.   Ensure you Note the style of the dial on a watch. The 'dial' of a watch is utilized to recognize how the numbers are documented outwardly. A few dials utilize numbers around the outside. This is known as Arabic style. Some others dials utilize roman numerals which is alluded to as the Roman style. While a stick style is spoken to by s Small straight lines rather than numbers.

5.   Ensure to take note of the style of tie on the watch. When making a watch you may likewise need to think about the style of tie connected. Most watches utilize metal ties or calfskin lashes. A metal lash utilizes clasped portions to frame a tie around the wrist. This is typically an intense tie, yet a few people think that its awkward. A few anyway lean towards a calfskin lash with a clasp to alter snugness, however cowhide has been seen as less sturdy.

FROM GOLD TO NIVACHRON

You should not have to have a financial plan to learn, yet the best possible devices for chipping away at watches are extravagant. You may consequently consider buying the hardware store of a resigned/perished watchmaker.

CHAPTER FOUR

HOW TO BECOME A PRO IN THE ART OF WATCH MAKING

Turning into a specialist watch creator may require some investment and experience. You won't need to make anything yet not until in any event a year into learning. In the event that you are modest or sluggish in learning you may not need to try learning. You should remember that a 0.5mm contrast in watchmaking is big, so accuracy is everything with regards to watch making. It requires appropriate instrumentation and tolerance.

With respect to planning and making your own development, you may initially need to find out about watches. Guarantee you don't skirt any means. Having somebody make your development could be over the top expensive. It is possible that they will do it by hand, or you should burn through thousands to make up for their work hours. Or on the other hand in the event that they do it by CNC, and you will spend at any rate 1k also for one development.

My watch ace has been into watch making for more than 25 years and still he has not made his own development without any preparation. It is certain a procedure that takes weeks/months/and significantly more particularly on the off chance that you are as yet learning. It isn't care for you simply purchase the apparatuses and begin making your watch.

A Guide to Common Watchmaking Materials

The craft of watchmaking will perpetually be attached to the hundreds of years old conventions. Be that as it may, present day watchmakers don't stop to adjust with the occasions.

As of late, some new brands have committed a lot of their exploration and formative endeavors to one specific zone of intrigue: the development of new materials for watch making. In the current occasions, watchmakers utilize all the more bleeding edge materials in their manifestations dissimilar to previously.

In those long stretches of early watchmaking, craftsmans meticulously created every single segment by physically. This proceeded till around the twenty-first century where these components were made of materials, for example, valuable metals, chrome covered metal and treated steel. Industrialization in the long run prompted bigger scope creation, which gave space for an increasingly proficient and less dull technique for assembling watches. This likewise prompted the advancement of new and better materials that assisted with supporting the productivity of the watch itself.

The utilization of a few materials in watchmaking surpasses the appearance of a conventional two-tone plan versus a cutting edge PVD-covered hardened steel. Different Brands are utilizing cutting edge materials in their watches from within to the outside. They give the model another appearance as well as help to expand sturdiness and lessen their loads.

CHAPTER FIVE

SOME USEFUL GUIDES TO USING THE RIGHT

WATCHMAKING MATERIALS;

From Time-Tested Standbys to The Latest Innovations. Watchmaking Materials may incorporate

1.   Ruby

In the twentieth century, watchmakers utilize characteristic gems as the bearing for the wheel trains and some different components defenseless to the most mileage, similar to the departure switch. These gems anyway can assist with lessening grinding and increment exactness. In the year 1902, a French physicist named Auguste Verneuil set up a strategy to make manufactured gems or rubies, which have become exceptionally helpful today in current watch developments.

2.   Gold

Valuable metals have consistently been utilized as a major aspect of watchmaking since the start of horology. Gold in all structures are reasonable whether—yellow, white, rose, and red — has been an excellent material for various pieces of the watch. The most well-known spot to discover gold is the watch case. Previously and even until the start of the twentieth century, gold was all things considered the most mainstream case material utilized for watch making. In the beginning of watchmaking, makers additionally utilized valuable metals, for example, gold in the watchmaking developments.

3.	Nickel-Plated Brass

As watchmakers extended and expanded the materials they utilized, they likewise looked to different businesses. Makers likewise have utilized nickel-plated metal for a few quantities of utilizations going from weaponry to fundamental stray pieces. Nickel-plated metal likewise engaged watchmakers because of the way that it was a more affordable option in contrast to valuable metals and hardened steel, and furthermore more erosion safe than metal. This absolute last quality is basic for segments of the watch just as their life span. In early timepieces, watchmakers utilized nickel-plated metal for both inner and outer components for parts of the development to the packaging.

4.	Stainless Steel

Watchmaker's likewise utilizes tempered steel for watchmaking, this has truly adjusted the scene of current timepieces. It has since made its introduction in the year 1930s and has since supplanted gold as the most famous and generally utilized packaging material for watchmaking. When Compared to gold, hardened steel is lightweight, consumption safe and exceptionally practical. The developing number of hardened steel looks out for time likewise mirrors the advancement of the watch's style just as the reason on the loose. Gold was an extremely fitting material when timepieces were all the more an adornments thing and furthermore superficial point of interest. In any case, today numerous watches are significantly progressively lively and furthermore utilitarian in nature and structure.

5.   Bronze

Bronze is probably the soonest material utilized by man, dated back to the mid-fourth thousand years BC. However, the deep rooted segment of bronze has as of late flooded in prominence among watchmakers. A few Watch marks at first utilized bronze for its utility. Bronze cases are extremely decent alternatives for plunge watches due to the non-destructive and hostile to attractive characteristics of the material. As of late, bronze watches have gone past capacity and has gone

work and has gone into style. The magnificence of bronze from a structure point of view is standing out it ages with time; its combination procures an unmistakable patina that is absolutely special.

6.   Silicon

Utilizing silicon in watchmaking has been one of the business' greatest distinct advantages. Watchmakers started completing experimentation with silicon near the new thousand years Since that time, numerous other watch organizations have step by step supplanted metal parts with the silicon, basically inside the whole development. Points of interest of Silicon over metal — it is lightweight, it is temperature obstruction, it is frictionless, and furthermore antimagnetic, it is more enthusiastically and more grounded than metal. The Silicon parts permit the development to run at a higher recurrence, it is a progressively precise watch.

7.   Ceratanium

This sort of crossover materials is probably the most recent pattern in watchmaking. In the year 2017, the main appearance of Ceratanium was seen from IWC. This combination for the most part consolidates titanium and clay. Rather than the different strategies like covering or plating, IWC really assists with holding the two materials together. The consequence of this is lightweight, consistently scratch-safe, and extra ultra solid. It is rich dark shade that doesn't look excessively decrepit on the wrist, either.

8.   Titanium

A very long while prior after hardened steel hit the watch showcase, titanium additionally became possibly the most important factor. In 1970, Citizen was the first to make a big appearance the material in a timepiece. In spite of the way that titanium was one of watchmaking's most agreeable materials (it is light), it has never become very as predominant as the tempered steel. It anyway shares a significant number of similar focal points, for example, being tough, and consumption safe. it is additionally increasingly exorbitant. However, there are various titanium watches in the market today. It is frequently think that its utilized in plunge and device watch models.

PVD and DLC Coatings

A few dark watches have been a pattern as of late. In any case, the different styles goes back to 1970s. The genuine contrast between the first passed out watches and their cutting edge partners is really the way toward acquiring the particular monochrome tint. Early varieties utilized a powder-covered paint that scratched effectively, which traded off the smooth look. Today, watchmakers utilize new procedures called physical fume testimony (PVD) and jewel like covering (DLC). The two techniques permit the watchmakers to include a slight, hard covering to hardened steel that is almost difficult to scratch.

Carbotech

A man named Panerai spearheaded a material called Carbotech a few years prior, in 2015 definitely. This ultra-extreme segment is typically made of strengthened carbon fiber, which makes it ideal for the brand's rough and utilitarian structures. The material's sythesis likewise gives it an unmistakable grain shading, so it looks similarly in the same class as it performs.

Carbon Glass

Carbon glass is another normal material that is new to the field of watchmaking. Girard-Perregaux is one of the first to utilize the progressive segment in probably the most recent expansion to their Laureato Absolute assortment arrangement. This cycle of carbon assisted with coordinating pigmented glass strands during a high temperature infusion. This came about to multiple times stiffer than steel watches and a genuinely exceptional look.

Nivachron

In the year 2018, the Swatch Group declared the advancement of a fresh out of the box new amalgam named Nivachron in organization with Audemars Piguet. This material was made the as an option in contrast to silicon for parts of the development, similar to the hairspring. Nivachron is known to have a mind boggling structure with a titanium base, which permits it to hold the pliability of metal amalgams while staying hostile to attractive just as temperature and stun safe.

CHAPTER SIX

BIT BY BIT GUIDE ON WATCHMAKING

MATERIALS NEEDED

The following are the devices required for watchMaking .

- Bench Mat

- Microfiber Cloth

- Rodico

- Dust Blower

- Finger Cots

- End Cutter

- File

- Sharpie

- Pin Vise

- Glue

- Hand Presser

- Dial Protectors

- Tweezers

- Movement Holder

- Case Holder

- Silicone Grease

- JAXA Wrench

- Spring Bar Tool

Stage 1

Draw out all the parts from your Make My Own Watch Kit and check with the rundown of the parts so as to distinguish every segment. Expel every development from its defensive case and put it into the development holder.

Stage 2

JOIN THE DIAL ONTO MOVEMENT

Guarantee you Line up the dial feet into the relating openings on the development. Guarantee you situate the development to such an extent that the opening for the stem is at 3 o'clock position and agreed with the date window. The dial ought to be clutched the development alongside the dial feet, which grating in. One or the two feet can be twisted, when that happens you would now be able to utilize forceps to delicately twist it back.

Dial Feet

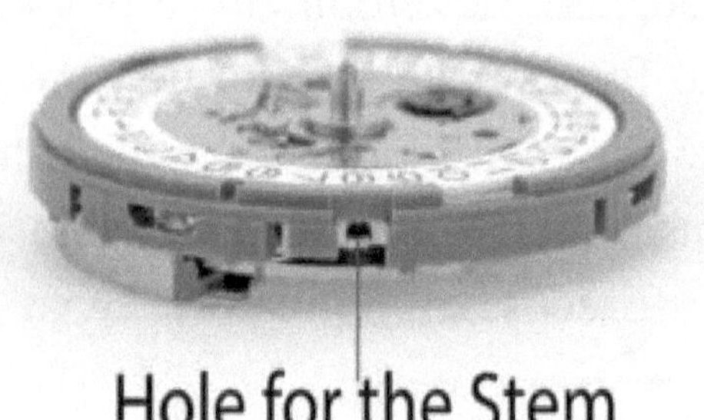

Hole for the Stem

One simple approach to distinguish the 3 o'clock positions from the highest point of the development is to search for the rigging. It is generally situated over the opening for the stem.

You might need to abstain from scratching and smearing the dial, so in this manner utilize defensive finger beds when taking care of parts. You can likewise utilize rodico in the event that you have to wipe or clean up residue or fingerprints from the dial.

Stage 3

INSERT THE MOVEMENT AND SPOT IN A CASE

Guarantee you Place the dial and development into the case with the dial confronting descending to the glass. Guarantee you line up the date window on the dial with the cylinder looking into it. At that point Place the case glass side down on a scratch free surface.

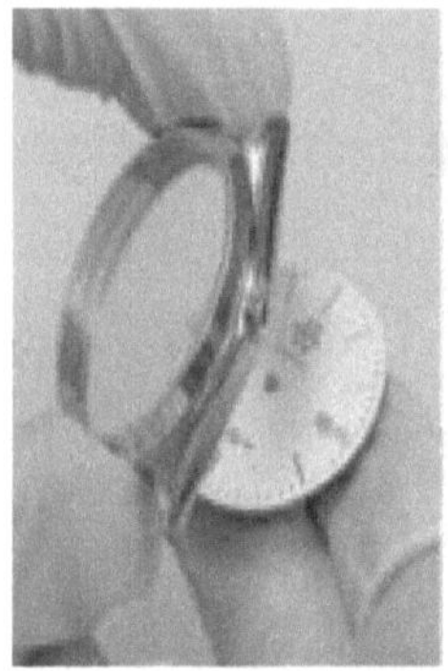

Stage 4

CUT STEM TO SIZE

The stem that generally comes in your unit is unreasonably long for the watch and in this way should be cut to fit appropriately. The stem likewise should be cut down to about 15.15mm in general length. Before cutting the stem guarantee you measure out where you will check and afterward cut the stem. Measure the stem utilizing a sharpie or bit of tape and imprint to the outside of 15.15mm. guarantee you don't stop the stem as well. Your pack accompanies two stems in the occasion the first gets cut too off is viewed as harmed.

The following are two techniques to slice the stem to measure. First strategy includes utilizing an advanced caliper is excluded with the Make My Own Watch toolbox and afterward the second is utilizing the measure that is incorporated with the toolbox. Guarantee you utilize a marker or bit of tape to check where the stem should be cut to.

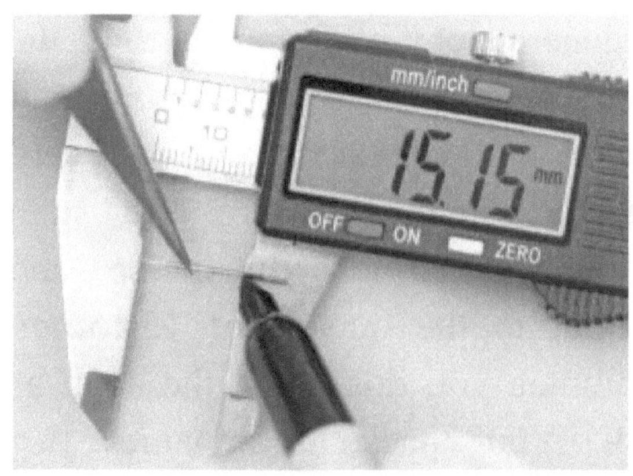

With the computerized check accessible, open it to about 15.15mm and lock it with the nut so it doesn't move. Guarantee you Use tweezers to hold the stem over the opening with the strung side going over the highest point of the jaw. At that point Mark the specific cut area with a sharpie or bit of tape at the opening of the jaw.

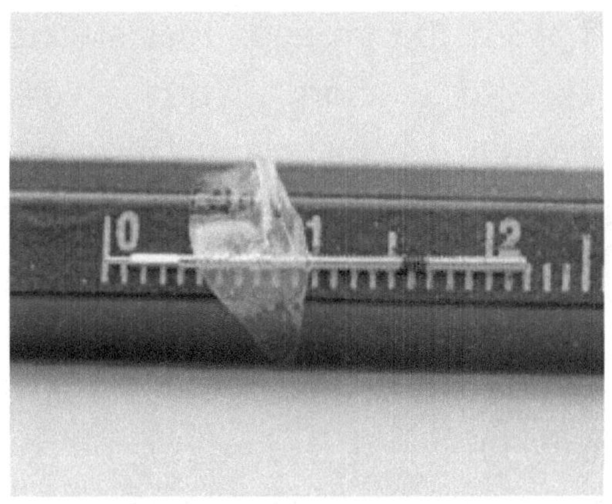

With the estimating measure found on the spring bar instrument, you can tape the stem to the apparatus to such an extent that the smooth end sits precisely at the center of the zero line. At that point Mark the cut area between the 15 and 16mm focuses.

You would now be able to embed the stem into a pin tight clamp and afterward utilize a side shaper, shear or end shaper included with the toolbox to remove the overabundance where you denoted the stem. We ought to Be mindful so as not to cut a lot off it on the grounds that a stem that is too short won't work appropriately. You can later cut progressively off the stem on the off chance that it is still too long after the underlying cut. Subsequent to cutting, there is constantly a part of metal left, you can utilize a record or bit of sandpaper to smooth the finish of the stem. At that point document the stem with the end opposite to the sandpaper for a level and even completion.

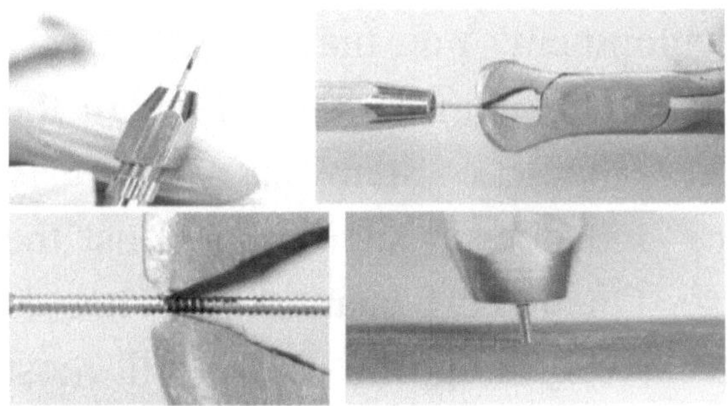

With the stem still in its pin tight clamp position , screw the crown onto the stem and afterward expel the stem and crown from the pin tight clamp and supplement them into the case and development in order to guarantee they fit effectively. Guarantee you Insert gradually until it is situated completely against the case and it fits properly.

In the event that the stem isn't sufficiently long, you may hear just a single tick or no snaps at all or it probably won't remain in the development. You may need to begin once again with another stem. In the event that the Stem is excessively long and doesn't sit flush against the case. On the off chance that stem is excessively long, the crown will most likely be unable to sit flush with the situation when pushed in. The watch will at present capacity ordinarily yet you may chance residue and water harm without fixing it appropriately. Evacuate the stem and scrape it down marginally on the strung end and attempt it once more. Stem is the real length and the crown is flush with the case. In the wake of affirming that the crown sits flush and the stem is at the correct length, expel the come from the development and discharge the stem by pushing down on the set switch dimple. The stem ought to be driven right into the development before you can evacuate it. At that point the dimple will show up behind the 4 o'clock position. Utilizing a sharp device, for example, screwdriver or pin pusher. Guarantee you press softly on the dimple and haul the stem and crown out of the development.

Stage 5

Joining THE CROWN TO THE STEMFirst of all you should Place the stem into a pin tight clamp and unscrew the crown. at that point place a limited quantity of paste or loctite into the strung finish of the stem at that point screw the crown over the paste the extent that it goes. You would now be able to put aside to dry for a couple of moments. Presently you should realize that the stem is at the right length and the crown is appended to the stem. You would now be able to remove the development from the watch case and afterward be prepared to introduce the hands.

Stage 6

ADJUSTING THE HAND OF THE WATCH TO THE DATE CHANGE

With the development and dial cooperating without the hands introduced, embed both the stem and crown into the development. Push the stem and crown in and afterward pull out on the crown to the subsequent snap and turn the crown clockwise until the number date begins evolving. At the point when the date divides any two numbers, quit turning.

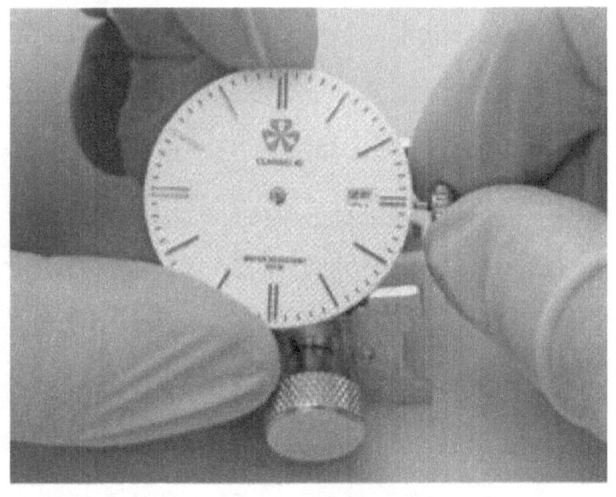

Stage 7

ADJUSTING THE HAND OF THE WATCH TO THE DATE CHANGE

Start by introducing the hour hand first then the most brief hand with the biggest mounting gap. Haul the crown out to the subsequent snap in order to prevent the hands from moving while you are attempting to introduce them. At that point place a dial defender to keep it from scratching. When utilizing the metal tweezers, guarantee you delicately place your hand at the 12 o'clock position in order to coordinate the date change. Hold up until the date begin moving once again to the following day around 12 PM. With the hour hand kept set up, use would then be able to utilize a 1.5mm (dark tip) hand press to push during the time hand over the post.

Rehash this progression for the moment hand, guaranteeing arrangement at the 12 o'clock position. You would then be able to utilize the 1.00mm (dark tip) hand press to press the moment hand.

Utilizing your metal tweezers, place the other hand on the focal point of the post. This assists with utilizing a headband magnifier to more readily observe the little post. At that point utilize the level end metal tip of the hand press to push it over the post; guarantee to utilize light weight so you don't twist the hands.

When the hand has been effectively introduced, at that point you should guarantee that they don't contact one another and are for the most part corresponding with one another and the dial. You would then be able to twist the hands marginally with tweezers in the event that they are contacting or calculated. Be extremely delicate as the tweezers can scratch and curve the hands.

Check the hands arrangement by hauling the crown out and going it to a couple of revolutions. At that point Push the crown in and wind for two turns and watch that the second hand pivots uninhibitedly around the dial.

Feel free to expel the stem and crown gathering from the development utilizing the put switch and set in a safe spot.

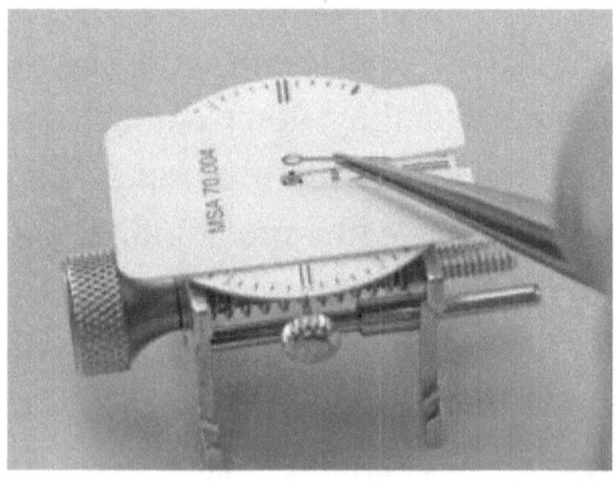

Stage 8

SPOT MOVEMENT INTO THE CASE

Guarantee to Place the development in the development holder topsy turvy so the dial is face down. At that point clean within the case with a microfiber fabric or potentially dust blower. Guarantee that no fingerprints or residue specs into the case before you place the development inside it. When the watch is fixed up, you may need it to remain clean. Feel free to Place the dial and development into the case with the dial confronting the glass. Guarantee to arrange the date window of the dial with the case tube looking into it.

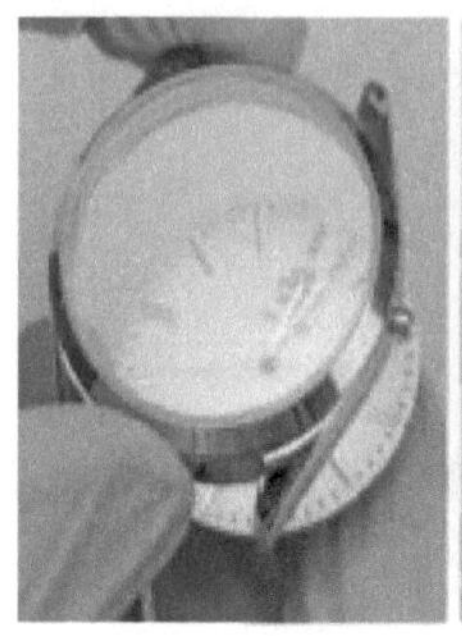

Stage 9

Introduce THE STEM AND CROWN

To do this, Put the stem and crown back in the development for the last time. Press firmly in until it fits properly.

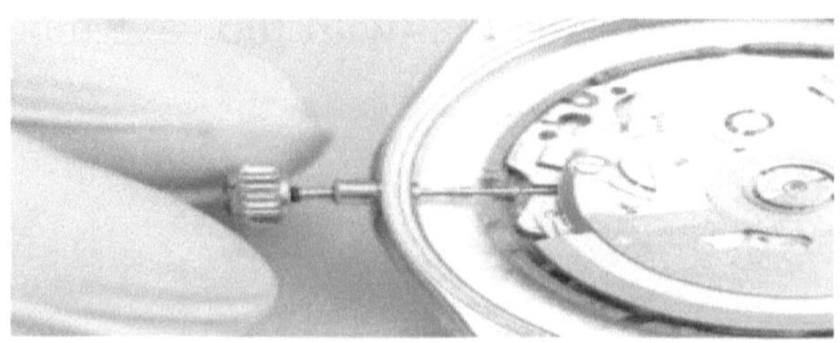

Stage 10

Spot MOVEMENT RING INTO CASE

Guarantee you Put the development ring over the development into the case. This ring has a pattern that must be lined up with the stem and the opening of the pattern must face the dial. On the off chance that you are not cautious about adjusting the pattern to the stem, you may harm the stem or case tube when introducing the development ring.

Press delicately the ring down until it is even with the case on all sides. Guarantee it is near a similar very tallness as the development and keep completely set up. The pattern of the ring as a rule fits around the case cylinder and stem.

Stage 11

Spot SPACER RINGA white spacer ring is expected to shield all the parts from moving inside the watch case. place the ring over the development ring, essentially into the notches. There is no base or up side, as it is a level ring on all sides.

Stage 12

PUT THE GASKET ON THE WATCH BACK

Grease up the back case gasket with silicon oil. At the point when greased up in silicone oil as required, the gasket will last any longer and be significantly less prone to spill in this manner keeping your watch development dampness free. This additionally can assist with guaranteeing that the gasket isn't harmed when the rear of the watch is in a bad way off or on for fixes or redesigns. Guarantee you don't utilize unnecessary oil, just a light layer is required. Guarantee you don't oil the case or back or different parts. A straightforward and simple approach to apply the oil is to put a limited quantity of oil on a paper towel. Guarantee to utilize the paper towel to grasp the gasket and pull the whole length of the gasket through the oil.

At that point slip the gasket over the side of the case back lip, hold set up with your thumb. At that point, attempt and utilize your pointer and furthermore the thumb of your second hand to loosen up the gasket somewhat to slip it around the remainder of the case back and furthermore fit it into place.

Stage 13

SCREW THE CASE BACK ON

In the wake of greasing up the gasket, the back is in this way fit to be put on the watch. At that point place the watch into a watch case holder and spot the back onto the case and fix it. Guarantee you hand fix however much as could be expected, subsequently utilize a JAXA wrench or other shutting devices to turn a 1/4 to 1/2 go to make it tight. Don't over fix it else it will be an a lot harder employment recovering the off when a fix gets fundamental.

Stage 14

JOIN THE WATCH BAND

Guarantee to embed your spring bars into the openings as a rule at the parts of the bargains band right through.

Hold your watch with the watch back confronting you and the crown to highlight the roof. Spot the finish of the spring bar from the band half with the clasp into the opening at the base carry. Guarantee that the watch band's done side is confronting a similar bearing as the face

of the watch. At that point take the finish of the forked of a spring bar device and push it down on the spring bar to pack it. You would then be able to utilize the spring bar apparatus to slide the spring bar under the carry and discover the opening in that. At that point move the watch band around the drags until you feel and see the spring bars jump out into place. Turn the instance of the watch around and afterward rehash with the other portion of the watch band.

Stage 15

TIME TO SET THE TIME

After your watch is totally constructed and fit to be worn, next is to set the time.

In the event that you have to additionally redone and customized watch by trading the band or the hands. You may need to include a date magnifier.

Stage 16

TIME TO SET THE TIME

You can set the time by utilizing the crown for the most part at the 3 o'clock position. It has fundamentally two setting positions; typically the first and second snap. So as to change the date, pull out the crown to situate 2 and afterward turn clockwise until the ideal date is reached. Next is to haul the crown out to situate 3 to set the moment and hour time. This should pivot both in reverse and forward to set the time.

In the wake of setting the time guarantee to push the crown back to situate 1 in order to seal the watch from residue and dampness.

You ought to consistently realize that the mechanical development in the watch is generally programmed and doesn't have or require a battery. By putting on the watch, as you move for the duration of the day keeps the watch wound and running regularly. On the off chance that you don't wear the watch day by day, wrapping it up physically can keep it running. You can wind the watch physically with the crown; while completely squeezed in then turn 20-30 times in the two headings. In the wake of injuring it enough to get the watch running, put on the watch and furthermore the auto winding component will keep twisting for you.

THE END